Monkeys

Lucy Bowman

Designed by Sam Chandler

Illustrated by Jenny Cooper and Sue King

Animal consultants: John and Margaret Rostron
Reading consultant: Alison Kelly, Principal Lecturer at Roehampton University

Contents

High life

Most monkeys live in the branches of tall trees. They are very good at climbing.

These vervet monkeys live in trees most of the time. They only climb down to the ground to look for food.

Tree to tree

A monkey travels from one tree to another by leaping...

...falling through the air...

...then grabbing
onto branches with
its hands and feet.

Monkeys have ridges on their hands and feet that help them to grip, like these dusky leaf monkeys.

Some monkeys can hang from their tails.

What to eat

Most monkeys eat food such as fruit, nuts and leaves, that they pick from trees.

1. A vervet monkey climbs along a strong, thick branch.

2. It reaches for thin branches, where the tastiest leaves grow.

3. It stuffs lots of leaves into pouches in its cheeks.

4. It moves to a safe place and eats the leaves in its pouches.

Many monkeys, such as this langur, eat flower petals too.

Land walkers

Some monkeys, such as these geladas, prefer to live on the ground rather than in trees. Ground monkeys eat plants and insects, and some eat meat, too.

A baboon eats grass near a large herd of gazelles.

A baby gazelle moves away from the herd.

The baboon gets close to the baby, then chases after it.

When the baboon is near enough, it grabs the gazelle.

9

Living together

Most monkeys live together in groups called troops.

Night monkeys live in a small troop of two parents and their young.

The troop sleeps in a hole in a tree. When it gets dark, the monkeys come out.

These vervet monkeys are part of a large troop.

They search through the tree tops, looking for fruit and insects to eat.

Some monkey troops have over a hundred members.

Territory

Some monkey troops guard an area, so other monkeys can't eat the food there. This area is called their territory.

Chacma baboon troops choose an area with lots of fresh food to eat.

They roar and fight to keep other baboon troops out of their territory.

When they doze, one baboon stays awake, in case an enemy enters the area.

Howler monkeys call very loudly. This warns other troops of howler monkeys to stay away.

Spider monkeys rub their smelly chests on the ground. The smell keeps others away.

Fabulous fur

Monkeys are covered in furry hair. It can help them in different ways.

Emperor tamarins have whiskers that can be long or short, white or yellow. This helps them to recognize each other from a distance.

The fur of adult silvered langurs blends into the trees where they live.

Their babies' fur is bright orange, which attracts other langurs to help with babysitting.

When uakari monkeys are scared, their fur stands on end. This makes them look bigger.

Under attack

Monkeys are sometimes in danger from other animals.

1. A troop of squirrel monkeys searches for food high up in rainforest trees.

2. A harpy eagle flies above the tree tops, looking for food to eat.

3. A monkey sees the eagle and calls out that there is danger. The monkeys run.

4. One monkey isn't fast enough. The eagle swoops and catches it.

Some snakes eat monkeys. They hide in trees, waiting for a monkey to come close.

Enemies, such as crocodiles and lions, sometimes attack monkeys when they are drinking at a waterhole, like this one.

Growing up

When baby monkeys are first born, they stay with their mothers for food and safety.

A baby woolly monkey clings to its mother's tummy and drinks her milk.

After a week or two, it climbs onto her back. She carries it around the forest.

As the baby grows up, it starts to eat leaves and doesn't need its mother for food.

When they are
strong enough,
baby monkeys
play fight for fun.

They make little noises to show
that they are just playing.

Monkey talk

Monkeys have lots of different ways of 'talking' to each other.

Monkeys comb through each other's fur to show that they like each other.

These lion-tailed macaques belong to the same troop.

Some colobus monkeys burp
when they are happy.

Blue monkeys make
different loud calls,
that mean 'danger',
'food', or 'follow me'.

Capuchins growl and
show their teeth
when they want to
scare other monkeys.

Baby vervet monkeys
make whirring
sounds when they
are upset.

Clever monkeys

Monkeys are very clever animals. Some of them have learned how to use tools to help them get food.

1. A capuchin finds a nut. It wants to eat the seed inside.

2. It picks up different rocks until it finds a heavy one.

3. It smashes the rock onto the nut over and over again.

4. The shell breaks and the monkey eats the seed inside.

Japanese macaques have learned to keep warm by sitting in pools of warm water, called hot springs.

Monkey love

Monkeys have lots of different ways of finding a mate.

Male mandrills use their bright faces to attract a female to be their mate.

White-headed marmoset mates stay together for life.

A male macaque gives food to a female, hoping she will be his mate.

A female proboscis monkey chooses the male with the biggest nose to be her mate.

Male baboons fight over a female. The winner gets to be her mate.

Not monkeys

Monkeys are part of a group of animals called primates. There are other primates that are not monkeys, but are similar to them.

Pottos wake up at night when most monkeys sleep. They live high up in trees.

Aye-ayes have long, bony middle fingers. They use them to scoop up food.

Lemurs have tails like monkeys. They hold them high in the air when they walk.

These are gorillas. They are part of a family of primates known as apes. Unlike monkeys, apes don't have tails.

Monkeys and people

Some monkeys are struggling to survive in the wild. People hunt them, or cut down the forests where they live.

These langurs live in a city in India. They find food there more easily than in the wild.

People are trying to put more monkeys back in the wild, by breeding them in zoos.

Troops of golden lion tamarins live in massive cages with trees to climb.

When the young are old enough to look after themselves, they are taken to a safe forest and set free.

29

Glossary

Here are some of the words in this book you might not know. This page tells you what they mean.

 ridges – raised lines on a monkey's hands and feet, that help them grip.

 pouches – pockets inside monkeys' cheeks. They can store food in them.

 troop – a group of monkeys who live and search for food together.

 territory – an area of land guarded by a troop of monkeys.

 rainforest – thick jungle that grows in warm, rainy places.

 mate – a monkey's partner. They sometimes have babies together.

 primates – the scientific group of animals that monkeys belong to.

Websites to visit

You can visit exciting websites to find out more about monkeys.

To visit these websites, go to the Usborne Quicklinks Website at **www.usborne-quicklinks.com** Read the internet safety guidelines, and then type the keywords "**beginners monkeys**".

The websites are regularly reviewed and the links in Usborne Quicklinks are updated. However, Usborne Publishing is not responsible, and does not accept liability, for the content or availability of any website other than its own. We recommend that children are supervised while on the internet.

This is a baby Japanese macaque. It is just old enough to eat plants.

Index

Acknowledgements

Photographic manipulation by John Russell

Photo credits

The publishers are grateful to the following for permission to reproduce material:
cover © **Cyril Ruoso/Minden Pictures/FLPA**; p1 © **2007 Kim in chirl/Getty Images**;
p2-3 © **RICHARD DU TOIT/naturepl.com**; p5 © **Elio Della Ferrera/naturepl.com**; p7 © **Thorsten
Milse/Photolibrary.com**; p8-9 © **Patricio Robles Gil/Photolibrary.com**; p10-11 © **Suzi Eszterhas/
Minden Pictures/FLPA**; p13 © **Piotr Naskrecki/Minden Pictures/FLPA**; p14 © **Jonathan Hewitt/Alamy**;
p15 © **Andrey Zvoznikov/Ardea.com**; p17 © **AfriPics.com/Alamy**; p19 © **Tim Laman/naturepl.com**;
p20 © **Koshy Johnson/Photolibrary.com**; p23 © **Morales Morales/Photolibrary.com**; p24 © **Pete
Oxford/naturepl.com**; p27 © **Eric Baccega/naturepl.com**; p28 © **Frédéric Soltan/Sygma/Corbis**;
p31 © **Yukihiro Fukuda/naturepl.com**.

Every effort has been made to trace and acknowledge ownership of copyright. If any rights have
been omitted, the publishers offer to rectify this in any subsequent editions following notification.

Sun, moon and stars

Farm animals

Elizabeth I

TRASH AND RECYCLING

Dogs

Horses and ponies

Spiders

Planes

Ancient Greeks

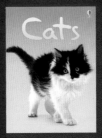
Cats

VOLCANOES

DINOSAURS

Your Body

Armor

Sharks

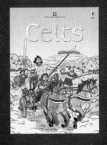
Celts

Vikings

Castles

How flowers grow

Digging up History

Living in space

Caterpillars and Butterflies

Ballet

Pirates

Egyptians

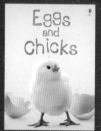
Eggs and Chicks

Romans

Weather

Tadpoles and frogs

Why do we eat?

Under the sea

Bears

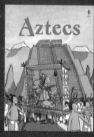
Aztecs

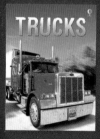
TRUCKS

Night Animals

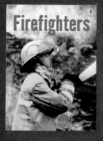
Firefighters

Antarctica

Bugs

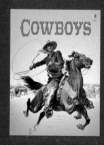
COWBOYS

Planet Earth